Hurt No More: A Collection of Poems
by Ziya Bates

Published by C & C Publishing, www.birthyourbooks.com

Edited by Tamika Sims of Get Write with Tamika ™

Cover design by Daisy Nkirote Mworia

Dedication:

To all the people who like my poetry, thank you, you guys inspired me to write a book. Mwahhh , enjoy <3

Table of Contents

Hurting

1. Sweetest Heart
2. Pennies in Cups
3. Burning Building
4. Without i
5. Like me
6. Lost
7. Naked Clown
8. Killed me
9. Worst Enemy
10. Loving You
11. Fuel
12. Proceed with Caution

◆ ◆ ◆ ◆ ◆ ◆ ◆ ◆

Healing Era

1. Swim
2. Lover Girl
3. The Line
4. Maybe
5. Here We are Again
6. My Best Friend
7. Stop
8. The Mirror
9. Another Life
10. Pieces
11. Joy
12. If i was a poem

◆ ◆ ◆ ◆ ◆ ◆ ◆ ◆

Happier

1. Forgetting You
2. More
3. Safe Space
4. Careful Fingers
5. Coffee turns Cold
6. I Wonder
7. Counting Moons
8. Love with a Poet
9. In-Between
10. Immortal Love
11. Stuck
12. Rollercoaster
13. Prove
14. Hallway
15. One Day at a Time
16. Society Bubble
17. Not Love
18. New Story

Sweetest Heart

"You have the sweetest heart," he says,
when I confessed my feelings for him,
I fancy him,
I fancy every detail on him,
his nose,
his brows,
oh and don't get me started with his lips ,
I fancy him ,
I fancy him a little too much,
I'm a little too much,
most say,
but he,
he said, "I have the sweetest heart,"
I overthink this to myself,
he said that,
he must fancy me back,
after I blabbered how much I long for him,
he let me down,
and left me confused,
he said I had the sweetest heart,
so he stepped and bruised it,
till my heart turned dark.
And now I walk with an unsweetened heart.

◆ ◆ ◆ ◆ ◆ ◆ ◆ ◆

Pennies in Cups

This poem is for the abandoned ones,
The ones who've been asking for pennies in their cups
for centuries,
But got none,
Oh dear little one,
When did things become so rough,
No ones head to lean on,
Especially when things got tough,
Oh dear little one,
Stop going around with your hand cuffed around a cup,
Asking, begging even,
For the slightest change,
When is this going to stop,
When are you going to stop?,
When are you going to realize that there's holes in your
cup,
So even when you ask for the validation,
 it still won't be enough.

◆ ◆ ◆ ◆ ◆ ◆ ◆ ◆ ◆

Burning Building

They say when you are born into a burning building
you think the whole world's on fire
Well that wasn't my case,
Everyone else saw the fire,
Except me
They stepped away for some reason,
Soon to find out from a burning survivor,
That I am the fire, I am the fire while I hurt you
countless times after you keep coming back for
more,
I am the fire while I transfer all my pain to you,
I am the fire while I burn you,
Each burn hurts more than he lasts,
Until you slowly can't take the burning sensation
anymore,
You leave, I don't blame you,
 Cause I am the fire while I sabotage myself

✦ ✦ ✦ ✦ ✦ ✦ ✦ ✦ ✦

Without I

what I'm about to say,
I say this with my whole life,
I say this with my whole being,
what i'm about say,
don't take it lightly,
"A world without people, is a world without me."
a world without people, the ones I love to the ones
that I don't, exist to,
a world without them, is a world without me,
a world without me, is a world to everyone,
because my problem is dependency.
I wouldn't know what to do with myself,
so i'll just sit quietly till the world eventually ends
me.

◆ ◆ ◆ ◆ ◆ ◆ ◆ ◆ ◆

Like Me

I want you to like me,
so I will form myself into another version of you,
starting off small, with my fashion,
how I talk,
changing my "wows" to "damns"
& you will like me then,
"like" is a understatement,
you will love me,
and all I will have left to do is
wave goodbye to the version of me
 that now lies in a casket.

◆ ✦ ◆ ✦ ◆ ✦ ◆ ✦ ◆ ✦ ◆ ✦ ◆ ✦ ◆

Lost

to be completely honest with you,
I am lost,
lost in a place that is truly familiar,
but I don't seem to recognize this feeling,
I don't feel at ease,
I don't even feel greeted,
I feel like they failed to salute me before the maze
started,
they were supposed to tell me about the expedition
that we are about to go on,
instead they left me alone,
in a maze, full of thoughts,
thoughts that were somewhat controlled,
now, now they are everywhere,
and i'm lost,
in a place that once was my home

◆　✦　◆　✦　◆　✦　◆　✦　◆　✦　◆　✦　◆　✦　◆

Naked Clown

naked clown,
two words I can describe myself as,
naked,
clown,
a joke being themselves,
where looking in the mirror and seeing myself
dressed up as a clown,
smothered in clown makeup,
that seems impossible to scrub off,
naked clown,
as I try take off my clothes to show the real me,
everyone stares and laughs,
as i'm just a naked clown being myself

Killed Me

want to know the heart dropping truth?
listen closely,
I died,
not with a gun in hand, point to my head,
but the day my body left my soul so empty,
was the day you left

◆ ◆ ◆ ◆ ◆ ◆ ◆ ◆ ◆ ◆ ◆ ◆ ◆ ◆ ◆

Worst Enemy

the worst enemy I have is food,
as it looks me straight in my eyes,
tries to intimidate me with its calories,
it works,
I fall right into its hole,
as I am puking, starving, anytime I can,
it becomes addictive,
while my heart craves for food,
my brain says no,
says no because it starts to see the potential that we
can get if we just keep carving,
deeper and deeper,
my stomach caves in, isn't this what you wanted they
all ask, I'm speechless as my bones clink as I walk

◆ ◆ ◆ ◆ ◆ ◆ ◆ ◆

Loving You

I heard our bodies don't know time,
So when you text me five hours later,
my body jumps for joy,
In hope for someone to love me again,
I gain nothing from loving you,
Although I can't bring myself to stop,
That's probably the worst part about loving you.

✦ ✦ ✦ ✦ ✦ ✦ ✦ ✦

Fuel

My body runs on others fuel,
Which means I'm nothing without something,
That something is someone,
That someone is you,
You are my fuel.

Proceed with Caution

Proceed with caution,
They say,
As I am entering this building that looks oddly familiar,
But
I don't quite recognize it entirely,
As i put one foot in, im extremely boiling,
Boiling in this so called building,
As I step my other foot inside,
I see fire,
I didn't know there was going to be fire,
I start to panic,
Soon the fire went out with the white foamy cream,
That you have to clean up afterwards,
And it took a lot of time to take in,
But this unknown place that I am in,
Is just my brain, my brain betraying me, my brain convincing me,
And I say, this is just the ordinary, the ordinary is my built of thoughts for the boiling feeling,
Fire is for the yelling that releases from within,
The blade is for the fire extinguishers that leave a bit of a mess,
So you have to clean up afterwards.

◆ ◆ ◆ ◆ ◆ ◆ ◆ ◆

Cares

cares, "it seems to be that no one cares,"
you said,
and as I begged you not to believe that thought,
the thought trying to bring you in the waters,
till you drown,
you have to kick a bit,
swim a bit,
you have to try a bit to not drown,
you have to combat those thoughts till you're
eventually on shore,
yes when wave come they hit,
but the question for you is,
Are you going to try and swim?

◆ ◆ ◆ ◆ ◆ ◆ ◆ ◆ ◆ ◆ ◆ ◆ ◆ ◆ ◆ ◆

Lover Girl

Italked to the moon last night,
I told them I'm a lover girl for you,
I told them I'm in need of your touch,
How touch deprived I am for you,
How no one's touch compared to yours,
No one compares to you,
I talked to the moon last night,
I didn't get a response back,
I talked louder till I was eventually yelling,
Cause I'm in need of my lover,
And they won't give them back,
As if my lover is held captive on the moon with no air,
no shelter,
I yelled at the moon last night,
I told them how I need my lover back.

◆ ◆ ◆ ◆ ◆ ◆ ◆ ◆ ◆

The Line

the line I wish you would say again,
just one more time,
another time,
the line that made me feel seen,
the words you said with so much meaning,
your lips whispered, "I see you like glass"
whenever I tried to lie,
because you know with your whole being,
that my favorite color is red but I say pink to strangers,
and how I'm a talker but I usually say I'm a listener because I'm insecure about how I talk,
you know me,
you know all of that,
because you see right through me,
I wish there wasn't a barrier in front of us now.
I wish I was still a looking glass.

◆ ✦ ◆ ✦ ◆ ✦ ◆ ✦ ◆ ✦ ◆ ✦ ◆ ✦ ◆

Maybe

maybe when the time is just right,
I'll be able to look you in the eyes,
and tell you everything is alright,
as if the world is not shredding into millions pieces
at once,
you'll be in the hands of the future,
you'll be in the hands of mine,
but for now,
i'll just have to look into the eyes of my mirror,
and tell them that it's going to be fine

✦ ✦ ✦ ✦ ✦ ✦ ✦ ✦

Here we are Again

and there I was again,
with my heart in my hands,
waiting patiently for one to come along,
and for us to trade souls,
in the midst of it all,
their souls shifts its look,
and shows who they truly are,
so,
here I am again,
with my bloody heart in hands
in mind there's regret,
I should've kept my heart to myself.

My best friend.

I am best friends with the sun,
I am their only friend,   .
most admire them, but aren't strong enough to go
near them,
with the fear that they might get burn,
but me,
I put my trust in the hands of the sun,
with their lonely beams of light,
that attracts me,
cause only a lonely being,
can know how it feels,
to be in no reach of beings.

"Stop"

one day I wrote about how i'm just going to stop,
stop trying,
trying my best,
because
"I have done so much running,
jus to find out that I wasn't even walking"
well,
that mindset,
killed me,
killed me to the point where trying wouldn't even pop
up in my head anymore,
I ruled out that option,
so today,
that mindset ends right now,
because trying and "failing,"
and trying again is how you get where you want to
be,
and if that means failing 200 times,
I know 200 ways not to go,
I'm happy,
or content at least,
and it's okay if I get in a funk again,
cause as I was told,
our life is like what you see on a heart monitor,
lines going up and down, up and down,
which guaranteed me feeling up again.

✦ ✦ ✦ ✦ ✦ ✦ ✦ ✦ ✦

The Mirror

While I look in the mirror,
As my reflection is telling me how ugly I am in ten
different fonts,
I chose not to listen,
I chose not to listen cause maybe I am pretty,
maybe I am pretty the way my lips are so perky with
my vibrant energy that flows within me,
and how my hip dips with a swaying motion as if I am
the ocean,
maybe I am pretty,
maybe I am pretty as I have my signature scent, I wear
day to day, so maybe i am pretty,
maybe I am more than pretty,
maybe I am charming, dazzling, with a hint of delicate,
maybe everytime someone looks my way,
I would have to say, easy on the eyes,
cause I am breathtaking.

✦ ✦ ✦ ✦ ✦ ✦ ✦ ✦ ✦ ✦ ✦ ✦ ✦ ✦ ✦

Another Life

Maybe in another life,
we will meet eyes and imagine the happy ending that
we didn't have,
but will this time,
Maybe in another life all the eyelashes I pick,
Candles I blow,
And prayer I pray,
Will go towards us in another life,
Maybe in this life we will compare this life and that
life and think,
"Wow! We changed but yet this feels the same,"
Maybe in another life, all the memories we made in
this life will
be equivalent in that life,
And it'll all feel ordinary.

✦ ◆ ✦ ◆ ✦ ◆ ✦ ◆ ✦ ◆ ✦ ◆ ✦ ◆ ✦ ◆

Pieces

They ask what's wrong,
As if they didn't hear my heart shatter in trillion
pieces,
Once I heard the break of my heart, I knew what time
it was,
It was time to pick up each piece
One
By
one.

◆ ◆ ◆ ◆ ◆ ◆ ◆ ◆ ◆

"Joy"

and she asked me,"What is your point in life?"
"joy,"
joy is the word that came to mind.
not joy to myself, but joy to others,
of course I like being happy
like is a understatement
I love being happy
I love when my cheeks hurt so bad from smiling
I love when I laugh so hard my stomach begins to
hurt,
not a bad hurt,
a good hurt,
but most of all,
I love bringing joy to others.
I love seeing them smile,
and they don't see the beauty,
but I see their beauty and beyond
I love making them feel safe,
as if I'm their home,
you can call me a people pleaser,
that's not true,
I just like making people feel at ease. <3

If I was a Poem.

if i was a poem, I'd be written in red ink,
and have lots of repetition,
for the circles I go in
each round I end up in the same spot, asking myself
where did I go wrong,
if I was a poem,
it'll be a
loud one,
rocky one,
have lots of hills and bumps, and lots of issues,
I don't know where to start,
if I was a poem, I'll be compared to the ocean,
when the ocean is still,
I am still,
when I say still,
I am alright,
but, when the waves come they hit,
it hurts, as if I am the foreshore,
if I was a poem,
i'll be a powerful one,
one that'll make you cry,
I guess what I'm trying to say is…
if I was a poem, I'd be a darn good one.

◆ ◆ ◆ ◆ ◆ ◆ ◆ ◆ ◆

Forgetting You

I don't remember your name,
After some years, some days,
I can't get my brain to register your name,
Your name, which I said on different days, in different
tones,
I don't remember our last moments,
But I hope I didn't say a promise,
The promise that I won't forget you,
Because I am slowly but surely forgetting you,
Forgetting your perfume,
Your voice,
You,
And I won't say I'm down about it,
Because believe it or not my biggest win was
my brain not remembering your name.

◆ ◆ ◆ ◆ ◆ ◆ ◆ ◆ ◆ ◆ ◆ ◆ ◆ ◆ ◆

More

There is more than life itself,
there are the birds & the trees,
that I find so interesting when there leaves turn
green,
there is more to life than you think,
not just a silly boy who isn't capable of loving you
back.

◆ ◆ ◆ ◆ ◆ ◆ ◆ ◆ ◆

Safe Place

to be completely honest with you,
I don't like the rain,
I completely despise it,
the loud thunder,
and the flashing lights,
I hate the puddles that creep into my shoes onto my socks,
I hate it all,
but with you,
it's a different tale,
with you I will sing to the thunder,
adore the imperfect lines of lightning,
with you I will jump in the puddle,
cause I am safe,
my safe place is you.

◆ ✦ ◆ ✦ ◆ ✦ ◆ ✦ ◆ ✦ ◆ ✦ ◆ ✦ ◆

Careful Fingers

"careful," are the words that lingered out my mouth,
careful fingers with my heart,
because I just had to glue on every component that
belongs to it,
just for it to function again,
careful fingers with my heart,
I say as I trust you with such a thing,
I don't do this for most people,
you're a special one.
so careful fingers,
clean hands,
bright intent,
because as I lend you my heart,
I cross my fingers this time,
And hope
careful fingers are dealing with my heart.

◆ ◆ ◆ ◆ ◆ ◆ ◆ ◆ ◆

Coffee.

This is a poem
for dark begins out there,
I know this must seem like the end,
But it's not my dear,
Coffee turns cold eventually,
It's only the beginning to a marvelous chapter
And chapter where you start anew,
A clean slate,
Because the past is in the past for a reason,
And you,
You are listening to me read this poem,
And you won't soon,
Because coffee turns cold eventually,
And nothing lasts for eternity.

I Wonder

sometimes, most times,
I wonder if the story never started,
if I didn't walk to the counselor that day,
I wonder,
and start to wonder why I wonder so much,
sometimes,
I wonder if I didn't tell them,
tell them that I wanted to be the next kid
six feet under,
Would I be living today?
most times I wonder,
I wonder so hard my brain starts to shut down,
as if I'm a machine,
wonder, if I could have done it,
done it without all the meds & therapy,
and blah blah blah,
sometimes, most times,
I wonder if I could've done it without help.

◆ ◆ ◆ ◆ ◆ ◆ ◆ ◆ ◆

Coounting Moons

1... 2 ... 3...,
I'm currently counting moons for you,
waiting for my love to come back with the affection
I've been longing for,
as if all the love I give, does a wrap around,
finding itself to me,
in hope for good karma to be real.

I was counting moons for you,
but somewhere in between,
wanting you & needing you,
I lost myself,
it seems that I was lost in the woods,
looking for something,
someone who wouldn't appear,
luckily I catched myself,
cause who wants to
be counting moons till they die

.

✦ ◆ ✦ ◆ ✦ ◆ ✦ ◆ ✦ ◆ ✦ ◆ ✦ ◆ ✦ ◆

Love with a Poet

don't be in love with a poet,
they say,
there lines will get in the way of your words,
as you beg them to stop,
there lines become passages of their thoughts,
that seems like they're flowing as if they're a never
ending river,
a never ending brain thinking thoughts,
don't be in love with a poet,
they say,
but fall in love with them,
I say,
let there limitless words creep into your mind,
heart,
and soul,
let them give you their heart in your hand and give
up forever,
cause listen,
if a poet writes about you,
you live forevermore.

◆ ◆ ◆ ◆ ◆ ◆ ◆ ◆ ◆

In-between

Somewhere in between the I love you's,
The air turned toxic,
To the point where my lungs were unable to access the clean air,
And the deadly breeze was getting to me,
The only way to get out of this hold was to escape,
I didn't want to go,
I kinda liked it here,
But I was dying,
So my walking turned into running,
My talking turned into silence,
Soon the toxicity turned into something incredible,
Something new,
Toxicity turned clean,
And I turned healthy.

Immortal Love

my love is like 1980,
like no other in this time,
my love is immortal,
never dying out,
others would describe it as unconditional love,
but I would say,
immortal.

✦ ✦ ✦ ✦ ✦ ✦ ✦ ✦

Stuck

stuck,
I once thought I was stuck,
stuck in this house that seemed to be on fire,
the heat creeping upstairs to my room,
I once thought I was stuck,
with no way out,
the windows were locked and hot,
no exits,
I once thought I was trapped,
so I made a hole in the wall,
and jumped out.

Roller Coasters

life is like a roller coaster,
I'd like to think of it as one,
endlessly going round about,
reminding myself that we are all alright,
see,
going up,
it's not too bad,
getting excited and overconfident,
this is my favorite part,
compliments, compliments,
everywhere I go,
about my bright red hair,
or it's my goofy self,
on the top is where I get nervous,
because it gets rocky,
I think of what over people want me to be,
going down its always bad,
as if I'm a on my way to the exit of life,
but then it tricks me,
cause we do it all again.

◆ ◆ ◆ ◆ ◆ ◆ ◆ ◆

Prove

I think I always wanted to prove something,
prove that I'm worth something,
something that's so expensive it's priceless,
prove that life is better with me,
prove that my jokes, my body, my love,
is better than everyone else's,
the best you'll find at the most,
I wanted you to know that life is miserable without me,
and that your mind start to run,
and your mind becomes your body,
and soon you're rotting,
but the truth is,
I was trying to prove the wrong person,
the real person I should've proved was me.

Hallway

I'm currently in a hallway again,
the doors closed on me,
which caused me to be in a empty hallway,
a hallway where I am constantly waiting for
opportunities to come,
a hallway where I am lonely,
an empty hallway,
you see?
the door I was in,
I was in there for awhile,
but no four walls are going to be forever,
no situation is going to last continuously,
which proves,
this empty hallway I'm in,
it's not for permanent.

◆ ◆ ◆ ◆ ◆ ◆ ◆ ◆ ◆

One Day at a Time

And she asked me,
How do you do it?
How were you so slow to pick up the silver
when everything went wrong?,
The words that came out my mouth were so simply,
Yet so wise,
I said, one day at a time,
One day at a time,
Just live today clean from anything,
Tell yourself maybe tomorrow,
then tomorrow becomes today,
And then today becomes one year clean.
So one day at a time,
I tell you,
I'm cheering for you in the background.

Societies Bubble

society tells you to love yourself,
be yourself,
well society shows me that I can't really be
myself without judgment,
they say show your true yourself in the nicest way and
then give you a face,
a face of pure disgust,
they think I'm disgusting,
because I won't sit in their bubble,
their society bubble,
they think I'm gross because I will not stand to be a
basic bum,
I make their hairs stand up,
I make them queasy,
I will not let them form me into what they say is
normal, typical even,
because I am beyond that,
I am on the flip side of normal,
I am unique, I suppose, I say to myself in the mirror.
.

Not Love

Oh darling,
you're not mad at love,
you're mad at what was given to you dressed up in
what you called "love,"
love is not cruel, love is not upsetting, love is not
confusing,
moreover, when he whispers so softly,
after sex,
that you're the one he "fancies" the most,
sorry to interfere with your so called peace,
but he is not in love with you.

◆ ◆ ◆ ◆ ◆ ◆ ◆ ◆ ◆ ◆

New Story

So here we are,
I tell myself in the mirror,
My life gone to dirt,
Without a warning,
I have to pack up my things,
My room, my life, my dignity,
Here we go again,
I tell myself once more,
New me, new friends, new beginning,
Let's make another chapter to this story.

◆ ◆ ◆ ◆ ◆ ◆ ◆ ◆ ◆